BRITAIN IN PICTURES

ENGLISH MUSIC

GENERAL EDITOR
W. J. TURNER

★

The Editor is most grateful to all those who have
so kindly helped in the selection of illustrations,
especially to officials of the various public
Museums, Libraries and Galleries, and
to all others who have generously
allowed pictures and MSS.
to be reproduced.

ENGLISH MUSIC

W. J. TURNER

WITH
12 PLATES IN COLOUR
AND
21 ILLUSTRATIONS IN
BLACK & WHITE

WILLIAM COLLINS OF LONDON
MCMXXXXIII

PRODUCED BY
ADPRINT LIMITED LONDON

★

PRINTED
IN GREAT BRITAIN BY
WM. COLLINS SONS AND CO. LTD. GLASGOW

THIRD EDITION

LIST OF ILLUSTRATIONS

BLACK & WHITE ILLUSTRATIONS

Illustrations reproduced by courtesy of the Trustees of the British Museum; on pages 16 and 27 by courtesy of the Curators of the Examination Schools, Oxford; page 28 by courtesy of the Trustees of the National Portrait Gallery; page 17 by courtesy of the Governing Body of Christ Church, Oxford; pages 44 and 45 by courtesy of the artist; page 46 by courtesy of Dame Ethel Smyth.

CHAPTER I

MUSIC IN ENGLAND

IN the sixteenth century England was known abroad everywhere as " Merrie England." In the nineteenth century it was referred to on the continent of Europe as " The Land Without Music." What was the reason for this change in its reputation? An enquiry into the history of English music will enlighten us because it will show the close connection between the life of the people and the music they make.

Music has been called the youngest of the arts by many writers in the nineteenth century, but in their search for sources they had not got much beyond the fourteenth and fifteenth centuries. European literature can look back to the great mass of Roman and Greek literature as a foundation, but no Greek music has come down to us. Many scholars think the reason is that there was no well developed art of music in ancient Greece. For example, Professor Sir Donald Tovey in the *Encyclopedia Britannica* writes :

> " the powers of music remain magical and unintelligible even in the hands of the supreme artists of classical Greece. We may be perfectly sure that if the Greeks had produced a music equivalent to the art of Palestrina, Bach or Beethoven, no difficulty of deciphering would have long prevented us from recovering as much of it as we have recovered of Greek literature."

But it is forgotten that music may exist before it is written down just as literature may. The Homeric poems and many of the famous Northern European sagas were passed from generation to generation by word of mouth long before they were written down. The classical Greek

7

writers speak so much about music that one cannot assume that their music was in a much more primitive state than their literature.

All music originated in connection with religious ceremonies and festivals. The break between Paganism and Christianity and the chaos resulting from the collapse of the Roman Empire contributed to what seems to be the new beginning of music in Europe.

We have no record of whatever popular music existed in Rome, and similarly there is no record of popular music either in England or the rest of Europe before the thirteenth century. Conditions in Europe prior to the thirteenth century were too troubled and confused, but from the thirteenth century onwards musical activity in England increased rapidly. Not only was there a constant outpouring of music written for the Church, but in addition there was a lively popular music. One of the earliest examples of this English popular music which has survived to come down to us is the round "Sumer is i-cumen in," whose date is about 1220. There were secular songs even earlier than this, such as "Virtute Numinis," an anonymous composition of about 1190 which is really a popular song and not ecclesiastical, in spite of its Latin words. Another early popular song is the "Angelus ad virginem," about 1318, and the famous "Agincourt Song," dated 1415, which was a song in English in celebration of King Henry V's triumphal return from the battle of Agincourt in France.

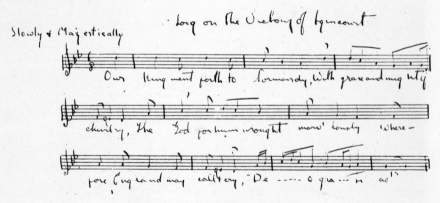

Our king went forth to Normandy
With grace and might of chivalry
The God for him wrought marvellously
Wherefore England may call and cry
Deo Gratias !

QUEEN ELIZABETH DANCING WITH THE EARL OF LEICESTER
Oil painting by an unknown artist

WINDSOR CASTLE : ST. GEORGE'S CHAPEL 1768
Water colour by Paul Sandby

Then forsooth that knight comely
In Agincourt field he fought manly
Through grace of God most mightily
He had both the field and victory
Deo Gratias !

Now gracious God he save our king
His people and all his well willing
Give him good life and good ending
That we with mirth may safely sing
Deo Gratias !

The powerful influence of the Church at that time was shown by the fact that King Henry V decreed that " no deeds sheuld be made and sung by minstrels and others of his glorious victory for that he would whollie have the praise and thanks altogether given to God."

About this period popular songs begin to be more abundantly available in manuscript. Many of them such as " I have set my hert so hye," " Now would y fayne summer this mak," " Alas departynge," " Go hert hurt with adversite," are still in manuscript and have never been published. In those days the English people expressed themselves naturally and abundantly in song, and in the following sixteenth and seventeenth centuries England became perhaps the most musical country in Europe. For example, Erasmus writing in his *Morae Encomium* about music of the time of Henry VIII (Queen Elizabeth's father) says :

" The English could lay claim to be the best-looking, most musical and to the best tables of any people."

This musical activity lasted until the rise of Puritanism, which began about the time of the Civil War which started in 1642. After the Commonwealth and the Protectorate of Oliver Cromwell the monarchy was restored. Charles II came to the throne in 1660, but this restoration did not succeed in really uniting the nation once again. Charles II had spent most of his life abroad and brought with him a number of foreigners, so that the Court was separated from the rest of the nation. When his brother, James II, came to the throne, there was a new revolution and James II left the country, whereupon William of Orange became king of England, and reigned jointly with his wife Mary, who was a Stuart. On the death of her sister, Queen Anne, another foreign dynasty came to the throne, that of Hanover, whose king became King George I of England. The whole of this period was most unfavourable

9

to artistic activity. The royal family was characterised at the time by the following rhyme :

> *King William thinks all*
> *Queen Mary talks all*
> *Prince George drinks all*
> *Princess Anne eats all.*

It is recorded of Queen Anne that she took no interest in the art or the drama or the literature of her day, but she possessed homely virtues. During the eighteenth century the split in the country continued, also the Puritan movement flared up again in the evangelical movement of the extreme Protestant section of the English Church under the leadership of remarkable men like John Wesley. It is true that this gave rise to a fresh outburst of popular music in the form of hymns, which proves that the natural musical inclination of the English people persisted. There was, however, no corresponding development among the professional musicians as the Court and society encouraged only foreign musicians. In time there might have come about a new unity of the English people, and a fresh development of its artistic capacity, but unfortunately this was hindered by what is known as the Industrial Revolution. England was the first country in Europe at the end of the eighteenth and beginning of the nineteenth centuries to develop the use of machinery on a large scale in industry. This development reached such colossal proportions during the first half of the nineteenth century that all the young active life of the country was drawn into it. It was not therefore until this process had begun to be slowed down by the rise of German and American industrial competition that a renewed interest began to be taken in music by the upper classes and the educational authorities.

CHAPTER II

THE DEVELOPMENT OF RELIGIOUS MUSIC

JUST as in earlier civilisations music was primarily associated with religion and used as an important part of religious services and festivals, so in Western Europe after the fall of the Roman Empire we find music arising again in connection with the spread of Christianity. As the Christian religion spread from Rome throughout Europe, establishing its churches everywhere, it brought with it the new Western musical art and with it the gradual development of a system of writing it down, that is, of musical notation. One of the authors of the Western musical scale was Ptolemy, the astronomer, who lived about A.D. 130. By the fourth century there was already an accumulation of music used in the Church, known as plain-song. St. Ambrose, in A.D. 384, put this into some sort of order, and similar work of co-ordination and organisation was achieved later by St. Gregory. The musical notation then in use was rather elementary, and the modern highly developed system of musical notation did not find its present form until about the eleventh century, and is chiefly due to a Benedictine monk named Guido of Arezzo. Popular music of the period from A.D. 130 up to the twelfth century has not come down to us owing to the fact that the people generally were not only unable to read and write, but were also, of course, quite incapable of writing down the music they sang. Just as writing and literature found a home in the monasteries during the so-called Dark Ages, so music also was only written down by monks for the use of the Church. Between the twelfth and fifteenth centuries the Church increased greatly in power and wealth all over Europe, and the art of music developed with it. It was indeed the sole patron of music and the sole employer of professional musicians. The only other music that existed was the popular music which mostly died with each generation, some fragments only surviving in the memory of the people. By the fifteenth century the art of music fostered in the service of the Church had developed to an extraordinary degree, and this is the period of the first great masters of European music. By this time musicians wrote special and very elaborate compositions which were more than mere service settings of the Church liturgy.

One of the first great masters was the French musician, Josquin des Près (1445-1521), who joined the papal chapel in Rome in 1486 and remained there until 1494. This residence may be said to mark the beginning of Rome as the headquarters of the European musical world. This was not due to any superiority in genius or numbers of Italian musicians, but to the fact that the Church was then the richest and most powerful patron of music and all musicians were dependent upon the Church for the exercise of their activity. They therefore gravitated from all parts of Europe to Rome. Since the Church was the great patron of music everywhere in Europe, musicians naturally went to the headquarters of the Church to learn their art. It may be said that at this period Europe had a unified civilisation, namely Catholic Christianity. Therefore the music written in Rome, Antwerp, Paris, Chartres, Rouen, Madrid, London, Salisbury, Winchester and Canterbury was all of the same character and interchangeable. The great masters of this period, whatever their nationality or place or origin, were all writing in the same style. To realise this fact we have only to make a list of the eminent composers of the period, giving their nationality.

Josquin des Près	*1445-1521*	*French*
Palestrina	*1526-1594*	*Italian*
Vittoria	*1540-1613*	*Spanish*
Orlando Lasso	*1530-1594*	*Belgian*
William Byrd	*1542-1623*	*English*
Thomas Tallis	*1515-1585*	*English*

Of the English masters mentioned above, Thomas Tallis, and his pupil, William Byrd, were both Catholics, and primarily composers of church music. Their works have been made known to some extent by publication during the nineteenth century, but there were a great many eminent English composers before this date, such as Cornyshe (1465-1523), Sheryngham (late fifteenth century), Fayrfax (died 1521), Benet (fifteenth century), Damett (middle fifteenth century), King

MUSIC PARTY AT WANSTEAD HOUSE
Oil painting by Nollekens

A FIERY SPIRIT

Masque design by Inigo Jones, 1613,
for Thomas Campion's " Lords Maske "

ENGLISH SIX MEN'S SONG

Manuscript of "Sumer is i-cumen in" *c.* 1226, now in the British Museum

Henry VI (1421-1471), King Henry VIII (1491-1547). Much of this music exists still, but only in manuscript, and is therefore practically unknown. The whole of this church music was choral, that is to say, for voices in unison or in part unaccompanied by instruments. The forms in which it reached its highest development were the motet and the madrigal. Both are elaborate polyphonic compositions written for

THOMAS TALLIS 1515-1585

voices singing in parts. From a musical point of view there is practically no difference between a motet and a madrigal, but motets at the beginning were rather more liturgical in character, and the texts were usually in Latin. As a rule they were written for performance on principal holy days, but later the word motet was used for any piece of church music of single design, regardless of the language it was written in.

The madrigal and the motet originated in Italy, but Flemish, French and English composers almost immediately followed suit, and nowhere in the world did the writing of madrigals reach a higher state of development than in England, where they were perhaps composed in greater number and variety than in any other country. There is an interesting description of the madrigal, written in 1597 by Thomas Morley, who was a friend of Shakespeare, and was himself one of the most eminent composers of the time. He says :

" Next unto the motet this is the most artificial, and to men of understanding, the most delightful. If, therefore, you will compose in this kind, you must possess yourself with an amorous humour (for in no composition shall you prove admirable except you put on and possess yourself wholly, with that vaine wherein you compose). So that you must in your music be wavering like the wind, sometime wanton, sometime drooping, sometime grave and staid otherwhile effeminate ; you may maintain points and revert them, use triplaes, and show the uttermost of your variety, and the more variety you show the better shall you please."

14

WILLIAM BYRD 1542-1623

Upwards of ninety-two collections of madrigals were published in England between the years 1588 and 1638. One writer asserts :

" While the Netherlands were producing little in respect of music, our own countrymen were eager with that awakened life and energy which pervaded the age of Elizabeth to venture into every unexplored region with a success which was stamped upon all their endeavours. The results of their labours are our inheritance to this day."

A foreign resident in England named Galliard has left the following account of English music at that time :

" Madrigals were much in use in the reign of Queen Elizabeth, in which compositions the English of that time had left proof of their ability even to vie with the best Italian composers. Nobody could then pretend to a liberal education, who had not made such progress in music as to be able to sing his part at sight and it was usual when ladies and gentlemen met, for madrigal books to be laid before them, and everyone to sing their part . . . but since the glorious reign of Queen Elizabeth, music (for which, as well as her sister arts, England was then renowned all the world over) has been so much neglected as much by the little encouragement it has received from the great, as by reason of the civil war, that at length this art was entirely lost."

Examples may be given here of the words of some madrigals. It must be remembered, however, that it is impossible to give in a few examples anything like an adequate picture of the amazing variety in

ORLANDO GIBBONS 1583-1625

form and character of these poems. If we remember that there are
extant at least one thousand English madrigals composed by musicians
of eminence, we shall realise how impossible it is to judge them by a
few specimens.

A madrigal set by Orlando Gibbons in 1612, by an unknown writer :

> *Fair is the rose, yet fades with heat or cold ;*
> *Sweet are the violets, yet soon grow old ;*
> *The lily's white yet in one day 'tis done ;*
> *White is the snow, yet melts against the sun :*
> *So white, so sweet, was my fair mistress' face,*
> *Yet altered quite in one short hour's space :*
> *So short-lived beauty a vain gloss doth borrow,*
> *Breathing delight to-day, but none to-morrow.*

Madrigal composed by Thomas Ford in 1607, author unknown :

> *There is a lady sweet and kind*
> *Was never face so pleased my mind ;*
> *I did but see her passing by*
> *And yet I love her till I die.*

16

FANTASIA IN THREE PARTS
by Orlando Gibbons

Her gesture, motion and her smiles
Her wit, her voice my heart beguiles,
Beguiles my heart, I know not why
And yet I love her till I die.

Cupid is wingéd and doth range
Her country—so my love doth change ;
But change she earth, or change she sky
Yet will I love her till I die.

Most of the famous writers of the period wrote poems which were made into madrigals by contemporary musicians and a very common theme of that time was that expressed in Shakespeare's lines :

Then come kiss me sweet and twenty,
Youth's a stuff will not endure.

17

With the accession to the English throne in 1558 of Queen Elizabeth (daughter of King Henry VIII—who was himself a composer) there began what has been always called the Elizabethan Age. It was an age of creative adventure in the whole of Europe in every sphere, and particularly for England. English ships began to sail all over the world, which was circumnavigated by Sir Francis Drake in 1560 In England itself there began to flourish a new art of music and drama wholly independent of the Church. Up to that time there had only been performances of morality plays at church festivals or associated with civic functions. Now an independent theatre sprang up and the works of the immediate predecessors of Shakespeare were performed in the university towns and at London. With almost miraculous speed this drama developed to reach its apex in the works of William Shakespeare, who was born in 1563, that is in the middle of this age.

The unequalled excellence of the English dramatic productions of this period by Marlowe, Shakespeare, Ben Jonson and others has become known throughout the whole civilised world ; but it is not equally well known that this enormous output in dramatic art was equalled by the contemporary output in music by English composers. If you read through the plays of Shakespeare and his contemporaries you cannot fail to be struck by the innumerable references to music. One might even go so far as to describe the Elizabethan period as music mad. It was the universal recreation of the people from the agricultural labourer to the Court and cultivated classes. The great mass of middle-class gentry, which formed the core of the nation at that time, were all brought up to cultivate the practice of music. The playing of viols, the lute and other instruments took place in almost every large house, and it was a common practice for the gentry to gather together in each other's houses to sing madrigals, glees and other compositions. This period has been called the Golden Age of music, but the whole of the English music of this period remains largely unknown to the general public of all countries.

Just as many continental scholars write as if the first literary expression of the Faust legend was made by Goethe towards the end of the eighteenth century, and are quite ignorant of the existence of the earlier drama of Marlowe, *Dr. Faustus*, which was written in 1588, so the marvellous compositions of such great masters as Dowland (1583-1626), Weelkes (1575-1625), Wilbye (1574-1638), Orlando Gibbons (1583-1625), John Bull (1562-1628), etc., remain even to-day largely unknown and ignored.

All these composers wrote numbers of madrigals in which the polyphonic art of music reached its highest point of development. There has been nothing like these choral works ever since, but they require highly trained singers to do them justice. When the Civil War came in England in 1642 and was followed by the rise of Puritanism, a great blow was struck to the old life of the people, and all this music greatly fell out of favour as the quotation from Galliard given above shows. In any case, no further development was possible along those lines. There was always a danger that this sort of composition might lead to elaboration and intricacy for its own sake, and this is exactly what happened. The work of the Flemish composers in this school of polyphony degenerated into pure intellectual artifice. In order to fit in with the jugglery of the part writing, such liberties were taken with the words by dividing them up into syllables for purely musical purposes that complete nonsense was made of the texts, and this went so far that, when sung, the meaning was wholly unintelligible and there was no real connection between words and music. The greatest composers in all countries avoided this danger, but that it was a common one is shown by the fact that one authority refers to Palestrina's famous Mass known as the " Missa Papae Marcelli " as being " a deliberate demonstration that a high degree of polyphony can be reconciled with clear choral delivery of the words."

CHAPTER III

THE DEVELOPMENT OF SECULAR MUSIC

IN addition to this highly elaborate choral music, both ecclesiastical and secular, which was being composed in quantities during the fifteenth century, there arose in England a fresh contribution to music in a profusion rivalling that of all other countries, namely, what are known as carols. These carols, which are songs of a freshness and directness of expression that can only be compared to the finest of early French, Italian and English lyrical poetry, were chiefly inspired by Christian ideas such as " The Nativity," " The Incarnation," " The Annunciation," etc. Hundreds of carols have come down to us, mostly anonymous, that is to say the original composer is now unknown. They are truly popular in origin and testify to the definitely democratic character of English music. The words as well as the music are frequently of great beauty, such as the carol " I sing of a maiden," dating from the fifteenth century :

I sing of a maiden
That is makeless
King of all kings
To her son she ches.

He came all so still
To his mother's bower
As dew in April
That falleth on the flower.

He came all so still
Where his mother was
As dew in April
That falleth on the grass.

He came all so still
Where his mother lay
As dew in April
That falleth on the spray.

A good example of a carol having its origin in the daily life of the people is one about harvesting written by William Cornyshe, who died

THE GORE AND COWPER FAMILIES

Oil painting by Zoffany

MRS., MISS AND MISS POLLY PAINE
Oil painting by Reynolds

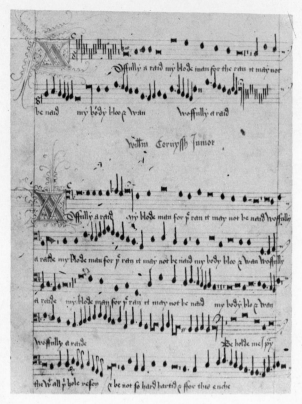

A SIXTEENTH-CENTURY CAROL
By William Cornyshe, Junior

in 1523. He was the master of the Chapel Royal under Henry VII
and Henry VIII. This is the poem, entitled " Pleasure it is " :

Pleasure it is
To hear I wis
The birdes sing
The deer in the dale
The sheep in the vale
The corn springing ;

God's purveyance
For sustenance
It is for man
Then we always
To him give praise
And thank him then.

Another very old carol of medieval times is " Cherry Tree Carol."
The words are as follows :

Joseph was an old man
And an old man was he
When he wedded Mary
In the land of Galilee.

Joseph and Mary walked
Through an orchard good
Where was cherries and berries
So red as any blood.

O then bespoke Mary
With words so meek and mild—
" Pluck me one cherry, Joseph.
For I am with child."

Then bowed down the highest tree,
Unto his mother's hand.
Then she cried, " See, Joseph,
I have the cherries at command."

O then bespoke Joseph
With answer most unkind—
" Let him pluck thee a cherry
That brought thee now with child."

" O eat your cherries, Mary,
O eat your cherries now,
O eat your cherries, Mary,
That grow upon the bough."

O then bespoke the baby
Within his mother's womb—
" Bow down then the tallest tree
For my mother to have some."

Then Mary plucked a cherry,
As red as any blood ;
Then Mary she went homewards
All with her heavy load.

Other well-known examples are " The Coventry Carol," " Good King Wenceslas," " I Saw Three Ships," etc. Carols originated as a sort of dance song performed at one of the great church festivals, but their performance was of spontaneous origin and not arranged by the priests, in fact they were often frowned upon by the ecclesiastical authorities as being of too secular a character. They also were introduced into performances of mystery plays which were so popular a feature of English country life in the fourteenth and fifteenth centuries. " The Coventry Carol," for instance, occurs in the Nativity play of the Coventry Town Guild. The first printed collection of these carols was published by Wynkyn de Worde in 1521. It contains the famous boar's-head carol which is still sung at Queen's College, Oxford, on the bringing in of the boar's head at Christmas.

An extraordinary wealth of folk-songs was continually being produced all through the centuries, and their melodies have often been used again and again by musicians of the nineteenth century (when they first began to be collected) and later. Such songs as " Waly-Waly," " The Cuckoo," and innumerable others are melodies of great and individual beauty. In addition there was an immense output throughout this whole period of dance music used in connection with Maypole festivities and Morris dancing. These dances, with their very strongly marked rhythms, have also proved a great source of strength to modern English composers such as Vaughan Williams, Delius and others.

The carol is a form of song, but while songs of all kinds were being abundantly created by the people, this form was rather neglected by

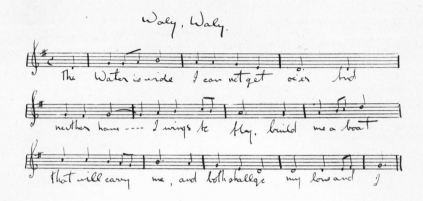

professional musicians trained in the Church. After the choral writing had reached almost the limit of complexity in the works of the later madrigalists, the professional musicians began to find a fresh inspiration in the songs of the people, and there arose a school of song-writers, of whom one of the most important was the Englishman, John Dowland (1583-1626), who wrote a number of songs to the accompaniment of the lute. There is a great wealth of such songs written by English composers in the time of Elizabeth.

About this time there began another development of secular music. The later forms of the madrigal and similar polyphonic choral music had lost all but their intellectual, one might even say, scientific interest. They had little or no emotional expression. Helped by the social development of Europe, a new form of secular music gradually emerged. As in all artistic movements, it is difficult to disentangle the purely musical from the social influences at work, but there is no doubt that early in the seventeenth century the influence of the Renaissance had

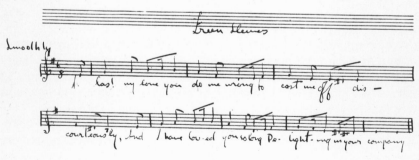

23

become so widespread and the increasing importance of the secular powers compared with the power of the Church centred in Rome so strong, as to decide the practical form of expression which music was to take. That is to say, music, instead of being a servant of religion became a servant of drama. All over Europe the kings, princes and dukes who were rich enough to maintain a court, encouraged dramatic performances for the entertainment of themselves and their friends. Musicians naturally were called in to collaborate, and this is how the new musical form of opera came into being. After the seventeenth century we shall find that all principal composers of every country, even including England, were composers of opera, and the quality and quantity of choral compositions declined, with the exception of purely liturgical work such as masses, etc., needed for the Church. Italy was especially favourable ground for the development of this music because it was cut up into so many small independent states, each with a ruling prince and a court. As wealth increased, it became the ambition of every prince to rival his neighbours in his dramatic entertainments, and the wealth of opera created in Italy during the seventeenth century is simply astonishing, and far exceeds that of any other country.

Monteverde (1567-1643) was one of the leaders in this movement, in spite of the fact that he was a church musician, being Maestro di Cappella at St. Mark's, Venice. Though he composed much sacred music as well as many madrigals, his real achievement is in opera. His first opera, *Arianna*, produced in 1607, showed the new idea which was to revolutionise musical expression. This idea was simply that music should express the emotional and dramatic value of the texts and that a composer dealing with a dramatic subject must find the single melodic line suitable to the character who was speaking, but speaking in music and not merely in words. Once it was understood that the music given to a singer who was playing a role or character in drama must be appropriate to the words that character was speaking, the emotion he was feeling, and the situation in which he was supposed to be, it became clear that monody (or in other words a single vocal line with instrumental harmonic accompaniment) was to take the place of polyphony. Up to this time those who listened to the elaborate madrigals and the motets of the polyphonic period could obtain frequently nothing but a purely intellectual pleasure from such music, but when the contemporary audience first heard the melodic lament of Ariadne in Monteverde's opera, *Arianna*, it drew tears from the spectators. This must have been

MAY MORNING ON MAGDALEN TOWER

Oil painting by Holman Hunt

A WATER PARTY
The Sharp Family on their yacht on the Thames at Fulham
Oil painting by Zoffany

DR. JOHN BLOW 1648-1708

a new experience. It must not be forgotten that the earliest choral works and almost all the works of English polyphonic composers were expressive and not merely intellectual, but the polyphonic form offers irresistible opportunities towards a decline into pure intellectualism. In England unfortunately, owing to the country being united into one kingdom with a single capital, London, and only one Court, conditions were not so favourable to this new development known as opera.

Nevertheless masques, which in the reigns of James I and Charles I (the immediate followers of Queen Elizabeth) were much favoured by these monarchs, are primitive examples of the new operatic form, and might have led to the establishment of an English opera rivalling that of Italy. An early English example is the famous masque of *Comus*, performed at Ludlow Castle in 1634, the words by John Milton, the music by Henry Lawes. Unfortunately the civil war which broke out in 1642 threw the whole country into confusion and disorganised all social life. The rise of Puritanism, which was to play such a role in the future history of England, was also an additional unfavourable factor. At the restoration of the monarchy in 1660, when Charles II became

King, there was some attempt by English musicians to produce an English school of opera following on the composers of masque, such as Henry Lawes (1596-1662), Thomas Campion (1567-1620), John Bull (1562-1628), but it was not successful for many reasons.

It is a strange fact that prior to this period (i.e. 1660 onwards), English musicians had been famous on the Continent, and many of them had held most important positions at foreign courts and churches. It was in the fifteenth century, as early as 1437, that an Englishman, John Dunstable, acquired a European reputation. Dunstable was a composer and a learned musician in the modern sense, and his motets are comparable with the best of his Flemish, Italian and French contemporaries. Another example is John Dowland (1583-1626), who was Court musician to the King of Denmark for some time, and whose music was printed, performed and admired in Paris, Antwerp, Nuremburg and Leipzig. Dowland was even described as the greatest lutanist of the world, and he was one of the best song-writers of his time. Another example was John Bull, who visited France and Germany ; at one time was organist in the Archduke's chapel at Brussels, and was in 1617 appointed organist to the cathedral of Notre Dame in Antwerp, where he died in 1628. Contemporary writers praised Bull as a performer of the highest class on the organ and virginal.

This international musical intercourse was all part of the general unity of Europe in religion, science, and art due to the twin influence of Christianity and the renaissance of learning. But about the middle of the seventeenth century this unifying influence had spent its force and disintegration had set in, and with it the first wave of narrowing nationalistic feeling everywhere. In England the restoration of a king who had spent most of his life abroad did nothing to influence for the better the general character of the country. The Court around Charles II was full of foreigners and gathered to itself all the more frivolous elements among the English nobility which rose in reaction against the fanaticism of the Puritan revolution. One extreme bred another. The Court and the nobility became more and more detached from the general masses of the people, and so a cleavage between the governing class and the mass deepened, and has remained operative until the present day. The consequence of this was that music in England separated along two different lines. Opera was fashionable at the Court and had no existence elsewhere. In spite of these unfavourable circumstances, England was still producing remarkable musicians. The most gifted of them was

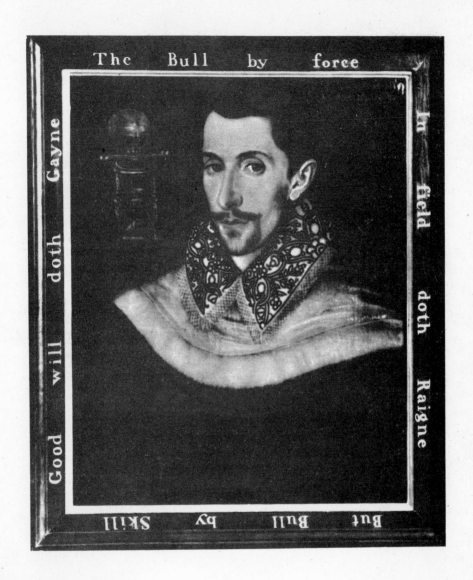

The Bull by force

In field doth Raigne

Good will doth Gayne

But Bull by Skill

JOHN BULL 1562-1628
Painting now in the Examination Schools, Oxford

HENRY PURCELL 1658-1695

ORIGINAL SCORE OF "BEHOLD NOW PRAISE THE LORD"
Anthem by Henry Purcell

Henry Purcell (1658-1695), who was a pupil of Dr. John Blow (1648-1708), whom he succeeded as organist at Westminster Abbey. Like practically all musicians up to that time, Purcell's early musical education was in the service of the Church. He wrote a great deal of magnificent church music, but it is in his operas that he made

29

his chief contribution to English musical history. Blow in his dramatic work *Venus and Adonis*, which he composed between 1680 and 1687, had made the striking innovation of having every word sung and none spoken. Purcell followed Blow's example in his opera *Dido and Aeneas*, composed about the year 1689. There is no spoken dialogue, but this is the only one of Purcell's operas of which this is true. Its place is taken by a recitative in which Purcell showed great mastery. He had the power of setting the English language with a directness and force due to perfect understanding of its rhythmic character. Purcell's recitatives have never been surpassed, and one striking example among many is the famous lament of Dido, " When I am laid in earth," in which both the recitative and the following aria are equally flawless in their direct and inevitable expression of the emotional situation.

Dido and Aeneas was composed for performance at a girls' school, and had there been State or Municipal Opera Houses in England for which Purcell could have written, this work would have been followed by other masterpieces. In spite of this lack, various actors called in Purcell's services to compose music for dramatic productions, and in this casual way Purcell was associated with the poet Dryden in producing *Tyrannic Love* (1687), *Amphitrion* (1690) and *King Arthur* (1691). In these plays the music consisted mainly of separate numbers, although occasionally there was some attempt at a coherent design. In *King Arthur*, for example, there is an attempt to confine the music to the supernatural elements in the play and to the lyrical moments. In this production and in the later *The Fairy Queen*, written in 1693, there was the beginning of a new operatic form had the social conditions been propitious to the artists. With the death of Purcell five years before the beginning of the eighteenth century the last hope of the development of an English school of opera was extinguished. The general social disorder consequent upon the flight of Charles II's brother, King James II, from England and the accession to the throne of William and Mary of Orange, followed by Queen Anne who died in 1714, was most unfavourable to artistic activity.

Unfortunately for England, Queen Anne was followed by another foreign dynasty whose accession to the throne of England came through a Stuart ancestor on the female side. King George of Hanover, who came to the English throne in 1714, was a German, who, like most Germans of that period, only liked Italian music. Throughout the eighteenth century German musicians (Mozart was a conspicuous example) had to contend against the prevailing fashion in Germany of Italian opera. King George I of England supported Handel and Bononcini and all the people of fashion in London naturally followed his example. London was a centre to which Italian opera companies came and stayed, and there was no longer any attempt at encouraging native opera. In the eighteenth century England was divided into the ruling Whig landed aristocracy, the Tory squires and a remaining mass of people insignificant in everything except their numbers. Nevertheless, in this mass there was a flicker of musical life in spite of the nation having lost its homogeneity. The descendants of the Puritans, who were now called Nonconformists (because although Protestants by religion they did not belong to the State church commonly called the Church of England), had begun to take on a character of their own, which separated them from the rest of the people who were in tradition or lineage descendants of the Royalists in the Civil Wars, and were attached to the landed proprietors. The Nonconformists—including the sect known as Quakers—were the forefathers of the industrial and commercial classes of the nineteenth century. It is my opinion that this regrettable division of the people of England, which persisted all through the eighteenth and nineteenth centuries, has been largely responsible for the musical decline during that period. A strong popular monarchy of nationalistic character like the Tudors might have succeeded in fostering the arts, but even this is doubtful, for the cleavage in the country at large had become too deep.

Nevertheless, folk-songs and folk-ballads lingered in the countryside, and even new ones continued to be produced. A popular dramatic form of music had long flourished, especially in Great Britain and other Northern countries in the form of the ballad. The ballad was always a story or legend in verse, and they are based on a few plots of universal character. For example, there is the tale of the girl who follows her false love disguised as a page, and is eventually recognised and happily wed to her lover, such as " Burd Ellen " ; there is the ballad of the dead husband returning to his wife ; there is the ballad of the jealous sisters, e.g. " Binnorie," which in one form has twenty-eight verses of which the first is as follows :

> *There were twa sisters sat in a bour ;*
> *Binnorie, O Binnorie !*
> *There cam a knight to be their wooer,*
> *By the bonnie milldams o' Binnorie.*

Many ballads refer to the untimely death of lovers and to ghastly murders and to drowned maids. There is the most famous of all ballads of treachery, that of Sir Patrick Spens, of which the earliest English manuscript belongs to the sixteenth century, but the ballad itself is certainly of much earlier origin. It begins with the well-known first verse :

> The King sits in Dunfermline town
> Drinking the blude red wine ;
> " O whare will I get a skeely skipper
> To sail this new ship of mine ? "

There are twenty-two verses in this ballad, which is one of superb quality from beginning to end   One of the finest of all the ballads, which is of Northern English origin, is " Helen of Kirconnell," which begins :

> I wish I were where Helen lies
> Night and day on me she cries ;
> O that I were where Helen lies
> On fair Kirconnell lea.

From a musical point of view one of the most remarkable is " Lord Rendal," which more than stands comparison with the finest dramatic songs of Schubert, such as " The Erl-King." Another typical ballad which occurs in various versions, Scottish and English, is worth mentioning, as it is of rather an unusual character. This is the " Twa Corbies," which I give here :

> As I was walking all alane,
> I heard twa corbies making a mane ;
> The tane unto the tither did say
> " Whar sall we gang and dine the day ?
>
> His hound is to the hunting gane,
> His hawk to fetch the wild-fowl hame,
> His lady's ta'en anither mate,
> So we may mak' our dinner sweet.
>
> " —In behint yon auld fail dyke
> I wot there lies a new-slain knight ;
> And naebody kens that he lies there
> But his hawk, his hound, and his lady fair.
>
> Ye'll sit on his white hause-bane,
> And I'll pike out his bonny blue e'en
> Wi' ae lock o' his gowden hair
> We'll theek our nest when it grows bare.
>
> Mony a ane for him maks mane,
> But nane sall ken whar he is gane :
> O'er his white banes, when they are bare,
> The wind sall blaw for evermair."

32

VIEW OF CLIVEDEN
Oil painting by Mercier

VAUXHALL GARDENS

Drawn by Rowlandson, engraved by Pollard, Aquatint by F. Dukes

From the Viscount Wakefield Collection in the Guildhall Library London

The finest ballads from a musical and literary point of view are the very old ones, but they continued to be produced throughout the sixteenth, seventeenth and eighteenth centuries, and even in the nineteenth century. Their real dramatic character, however, had been lost. The highwayman took the place of the knights and ladies of the Middle Ages, and the general tone became much less grim and austere. Even in the time of Queen Elizabeth the ballad had lost its old savagery, and a typical ballad of that period is one about the recently introduced tobacco, of which I quote the following lines :

> *Tobacco, Tobacco,*
> *Sing sweetly for tobacco !*
> *Tobacco is like love,*
> *O love it,*
> *For you see I will prove it.*

As the ballad declined, it lost more and more of its dramatic character and became lyrical and descriptive. Nevertheless it provided a great deal of material for which a new use was soon to be found. The life of the people began to reassert itself even in the cities, and in 1728 there was performed for the first time in London a ballad opera entitled *The Beggars' Opera*, written by John Gay, which ran for sixty-three nights with enormous success. This ballad opera, which was the most famous of its kind, but had predecessors and many successors in its genre, was both in subject matter and treatment far removed from what has been called " The heroics, the crinoline goddesses and ostrich-plumed monarchs of the Italian Opera."

THE BEGGARS' OPERA
After an oil painting by Hogarth

The subject matter of ballad opera is the day-to-day life of the country people such as one might meet any day on a village green in eighteenth-century England, and these people are made to sing their own music—ballads, folk songs and traditional tunes. The form is very primitive, more so than that of the operas of Purcell, such as *The Fairy Queen*, for the play is complete in itself ; there is no recitative, but the dialogue is always spoken and the musical numbers are quite separate from it. Even the lyrics are generally fitted to existing tunes, and it was only in this way that many English folk-songs were preserved. The musical outlook of the cultured classes at that time was so narrow that folk music was held in contempt, or utterly ignored, and it was not until comparatively late in the nineteenth century that English musicians began to see any virtue in their own folk music and to try to collect it.

The first ballad opera was *The Gentle Shepherd*, written by the Scottish poet, Allan Ramsay, in 1725, and the music of this work

34

was composed entirely of Scottish ballads. In *The Beggars' Opera* there are fifty tunes taken from English, Scottish and Irish folk music, but some of the music in the later ballad operas was taken from Purcell, Eccles and other seventeenth-century English composers. The first English composer of the eighteenth century to make an important original contribution to this type of opera was Thomas Arne (1710-1778). Arne was born in London and educated at Eton, and produced his famous ballad opera, *Love in a Village*, in 1762. The date is the more interesting because it is only ten years later than the first production, in 1752, of

P.H.A.Willis.

JOHN GAY 1685-1732

Rousseau's famous operetta, *Devin du Village*, at Fontainebleau. In *Love in a Village* seventeen out of the forty-two airs are composed by Arne himself. Arne had many successors, the most prominent of whom are Charles Dibdin (1745-1814), author of *The Quaker* (1775), *The Water Man* (1774), etc.; Stephen Storace (1763-1796), author of *The Pirates* (1792); William Boyce (1710-1779) author of *The Shepherd's Lottery* (1751); Henry Carey (1690-1743) and James Hook (1746-1827). The latter is said to have composed two thousand songs as well as innumerable cantatas and ballad operas, and from 1789 to 1820 he was the official composer at the pleasure gardens of Marylebone and Vauxhall, where eighteenth-century Londoners spent their summer afternoons and evenings.

During the eighteenth and the first half of the nineteenth centuries there was an enormous expansion of sea-going commerce in British

35

THOMAS ARNE 1710-1778

ships all over the world. For the greater part of this period this sea-
going trade was borne by sailing ships, and the voyages were naturally
very long, lasting from six months to several years. This life at sea produced a folk music of a character unlike anything that had existed before.
It was music sung usually by a solo voice with a chorus in which all
the sailors joined. Nobody knows how this music originated, but it
quickly spread from ship to ship and was universal throughout the
merchant service. These songs were called sea shanties, and every sailing
vessel had its shanty-man, who was the most naturally musical sailor
on board able to sing the solo part. The shanties were sung at work
and not during hours of leisure, and they were classified as capstan,
halliards, etc., shanties.

They were sung with great expression and rhythmic freedom, and
the origin both of the words and the music and the tunes is unknown.
The words varied a good deal from ship to ship and are as a rule altogether inferior to the music. This is an interesting bit of evidence that

EARLY VERSION
OF THE NATIONAL ANTHEM
in Dr. Arne's handwriting, 1745

RULE BRITANNIA
Words by James Thomson.   Music by Dr. Arne

37

A CONTEMPORARY SONG IN PRAISE OF SADLER'S WELLS MUSIC ROOM
In 1746 as it then appeared. Engraving by Bickham

the musical faculty is more innate and independent of cultivation than the literary faculty. In other words, it is more difficult for illiterate men to find adequate words to express themselves than it is for them to find tunes.

One of the finest shanties is " Lowlands Away," which was sung at the windlass and capstan. It was always sung with great solemnity and pathos. The use of the word " dollar " in this song arises from ships in the cotton trade with the Southern states of America. The reference to the sailor's true love appearing to him in his sleep is a sign of English North Country origin since the theme of a dead lover appearing in the night to the beloved is very common in those parts. These references indicate what a medley of influences went to make up these sea shanties.

Lowlands, Lowlands,
Away my John,
Lowlands away
I heard them say,
My dollar and a half a day.
A dollar and a half a day is a Hoosier's pay.
Lowlands, Lowlands,
Away my John.
All in the night my true love came.
Lowlands, Lowlands, away my John.

All in the night my true love came.
My dollar and a half a day.
She came to me all in my sleep,
My dollar and a half a day.
And her eyes were white my love,
Lowlands, Lowlands, away my John.
And then I knew my love was dead,
Lowlands, Lowlands, away my John.
And then I knew my love was dead,
My dollar and a half a day.

Shanties are usually solemn and full of pathos, or grim and very lively. Two famous shanties of the latter type are the following :

HANGING JOHNNY

Oh they call me hanging Johnny;
Away boys, away.
They says I hangs for money;
Oh hang, boys, hang.

And first I hanged my daddy;
Away boys, away.
And first I hanged my daddy;
Oh hang, boys, hang.   (Etc.)

We'll hang and haul together ;
Away boys; away.
We'll haul for better weather;
Oh hang, boys, hang.

WHISKY JOHNNY

Oh whisky is the life of man.
Whisky Johnny.
Oh whisky is the life of man.
Whisky for my Johnny.

JAMES HOOK   1746-1827

Although I have given these few examples of the words of famous shanties, the reader must be warned against judging them by their words. They have a unique character when sung and there is no other country in the world that possesses this sort of popular music. When steamships superseded sailing vessels, the type of sailor and his conditions of work changed to such an extent that shanties died out, and ceased to be produced about 1870. Just about this time, they began to be collected and we owe their preservation to various seamen with musical knowledge such as Captain W. B. Whall, whose book *Sea Songs, Ships and Shanties* is one of the first authorities on the subject.

There is another form of music which is peculiar to England, and that is the round or catch. It has been described as " a species of canon in the unison so called because the performers begin the melody at regular rhythmical periods and return from the conclusion to its commencement so that it continually passes round and round." " Sumer is i-cumen in " is the earliest example of a round.

At one time, the terms catch and round were synonymous, but the term catch is now applied to that kind of round where the melody is broken, and the song is interrupted in one part and caught up again in another. This rather crude form of humour or catch developed after the Restoration in the later seventeenth century. Rounds and catches were very popular all through the sixteenth and seventeenth centuries. The earliest printed collections of rounds was published in 1609 by Ravenscroft under the title of *Pammelia, Musicke's Miscellanie ; or mixed varieties of pleasing Roundelays and delightful Catches of two, four, five, six, seven, eight, nine, ten parts in one.* The term " ale house catches " is very common in seventeenth and eighteenth century literature, and this form of musical composition continued to be written during the

THE HARMONIC INSTITUTION

Engraved by William Wallis after T. H. Shepherd, 1828

THE BALLET NOCTURNE MUSIC BY DELIUS
Painting in gouache and tempera by T. Lee-Elliott

CANTERBURY CATCH CLUB
Early 19th century lithograph

eighteenth and nineteenth century. One of the most popular composers
of the later period was Henry Harrington (1727-1816), whose rounds are
notable for originality and humour. An excellent example of the latter
type is his famous round "Look neighbour look," which represents three
old women in a churchyard deciphering the inscription on a tombstone.

E

CHAPTER IV

THE REVIVAL OF MUSIC

D URING the Napoleonic wars a wave of patriotism and nationalistic fervour resulted in a great outburst of popular ballads and
ballad music, but this music lived and died with the life of the people,
and received no encouragement from the governing class which remained
largely immersed in sporting activities. It was also without any leadership from professional musicians patronised by the reigning sovereigns
and their courts. The rapid rise of industrialism at the beginning of
the nineteenth century spread not only its literal fog over large portions
of the English countryside, especially in the Midlands, but also benumbed
the minds of the people and most of their leaders. Nevertheless, the
increasing material comfort was a stimulant to artistic demands, and
during the first half of the nineteenth century there was considerable
musical activity in the British Isles.

Poets such as Robert Burns, the Scotsman, and Thomas Moore, the
Irishman, began to write new words to many of the old songs. One
of the most famous of Burns's poems written to an old tune is the one
beginning " My love is like a red, red rose." A famous song of Moore's
entitled " The Harp that once through Tara's Halls " is also written
to an old tune, and here is one stanza :

> No more to chiefs and ladies bright
> The harp of Tara swells,
> The chord alone that breaks at night
> Its tale of ruin tells.
> Thus freedom now so seldom wakes,
> The only throb she gives
> Is when some heart indignant breaks
> To show that still she lives.

This sort of ballad song and even an occasional dramatic ballad in the old sense are still being produced here and there in Great Britain, and it was the ambition of the famous Irish poet, W. B. Yeats, to revive this form of popular art. He himself wrote many ballads and stimulated other English and Irish poets to do the same. Some of them have been put to music by various composers, but it has proved extremely difficult to find composers who could do justice to the words. All these efforts, however, were rather an attempt to re-create the ballad from above. A genuine and inspired popular music can only come direct from the life of the people, and so far, the intense industrialisation of Great Britain in the twentieth century has proved unfavourable to the creation of any popular musical art. But it would be untrue to say that there was no popular music made from the beginning of the nineteenth century to the beginning of the twentieth, for a proof that it is impossible to suppress the vitality of a whole nation is shown by the rise during this period of what was known in England as " Music Halls." These institutions existed in numbers in every big town, and their mainstay was the comedian whose chief asset was his songs, both comic and sentimental. These songs were produced in enormous quantities, generally by talented men who had had little or no musical training. Some of these songs, especially the comic ones, were of considerable merit, but it is significant that the grotesque, satirical or purely comic songs were always far superior to the sentimental ones.

It is a striking fact that, during the latter part of this period particularly, the life of the people seems to have been such that no sincere emotional expression was possible. This tendency became much accentuated during the first quarter of the twentieth century. The love song, as it has been known in the past, has entirely disappeared, and its place has been taken by a cheap imitation of the negroid sentimental ditties of America. The total absence of sincerity and passion in the popular music of the twentieth century is a most striking phenomenon, but we are too near to it at present to grasp fully its significance.

The academic musicians of the nineteenth century were still under the influence of Handel, and most of their productions were confined to oratorios, to be sung at church festivals, and these oratorios were generally more or less competent imitations of Haydn and Handel. The country still produced musicians with talent, such as John Field (1782-1837) who was a remarkable pianist and toured foreign capitals and had great successes in St. Petersburg where he lived for some time. As a composer

VAUGHAN WILLIAMS b. 1872

he was a precursor of Chopin. Another prominent figure has been mentioned here, the Irish poet Thomas Moore (1779-1852), a friend of Byron, whose " Irish Melodies " (1809) was an outstanding achievement. Actually Moore wrote new words to old Irish tunes and was not a composer, but he was a means of preserving a great quantity of beautiful old popular music. Among the church musicians of the period the two Wesleys, Samuel (1766-1837) and S. S. Wesley (1810-1876) showed that the long tradition of church musicians was still unbroken. But in spite of such names as these and that of Sir Henry Bishop (1786-1855), English music was at its nadir, and the change for the better did not take place until late in the nineteenth century. Two important schools of music were opened in London, the Royal Academy of Music and the Royal College of Music, and a number of talented professionals came out of both these schools. There had also been, during this century, a great development of amateur choral societies, and compared with other countries amateur music was more abundant and more important than professional music. This was wholly due to the intense commercialism of the nineteenth century and the short-sighted utilitarian philosophy which made fathers compel their sons who showed any signs of musical or other gifts to go into business. In the country, however, and even in the big industrial towns, many amateur musical festivals were held. There are still innumerable choirs scattered all over England. Almost every small town has its choral society, and in this respect England is much richer than any other country. It is easy to find in any part of England a well-trained choir capable of singing important choral works, and Wales is even richer than England in this respect. Musical developments progressed rapidly from about 1880 onwards. Such composers as Parry (1848-1918), Stanford (1852-1934) and Edward Elgar (1857-1934) began to take a more important place in the European musical history of the period. Social conditions and the over-centralisation of life in London prevented the growth, however, of any opera such as existed in Germany and Italy, but Sullivan (1862-1900) became famous throughout the world with his collaborator, W. S. Gilbert, as author of a series of light operas, which to some extent may be said to have been derived from the ballad operas of the eighteenth century.

This musical development which took place in the latter part of the nineteenth century continued at an accelerated pace during the twentieth century. It can be said that since the beginning of the twentieth century there has been a genuine renaissance of music in England. The country

EDWARD ELGAR 1857-1934

still suffers from its over-centralisation in London, but the quantity of musical activity in London and the provinces is now prodigious. For more than forty-five years regular Promenade concerts at cheap prices have been held at the Queen's Hall, London, conducted by Sir Henry Wood. They continued unbroken, even during the war of 1914-1918. They are held nightly, generally for a period of from six to eight weeks, and are attended by thousands of Londoners during the holiday season from August to October. Although these concerts are called " popular," the programmes are made up of at least seventy-five per cent of the finest classical music of all countries, so that they have been of very great educational value to several generations of Londoners. The London musical festivals between the end of the war of 1914-1918, and the beginning of the war in September 1939, became the most important in the world. Not only was London the principal centre of musical activity in Europe, but English composers began to wrest the musical leadership from their continental colleagues. Delius

45

ETHEL SMYTH b. 1858
singing at the piano

(1863-1934), Holst (1874-1934), Arthur Bliss (born 1891), Benjamin Britten (born 1913), Vaughan Williams (born 1872), William Walton (born 1902) and Peter Warlock (1894-1931) are all composers whose works are as important as those of their continental contemporaries.

Delius studied in Leipzig and was a contemporary of the Finnish composer, Sibelius, but in spite of his German education, he was most influenced by the French impressionistic school, particularly by Debussy. His music is notable for its beautiful harmonic effects but is rather weak in structure.

Holst, who began his career as a trombone player in an English orchestra, composed in a more formal conventional style. His most popular work was the large scale symphonic suite " The Planets," which revealed him as a master of orchestral colour with great rhythmic vitality. His operas and songs have also won appreciation. Arthur Bliss belongs to the younger school that first came into prominence immediately after the war of 1914-18. He wrote a " Colour " symphony, which attracted considerable attention. Like most contemporary composers, the emphasis in his music is on rhythm. One of his most recent compositions, a ballet entitled " Checkmate," was written for Sadler's Wells theatre, and has had great success there.

Benjamin Britten studied at the Royal College of Music and was also a pupil of the well-known English musician, Frank Bridge, to whom he confesses a great debt of gratitude. His " Variations on a theme of Frank Bridge " was one of his first works to attract attention. His style is modern, but not extravagantly so, and he seems to have a genuine invention which separates him from many contemporary young composers whose music strikes one as wholly " made." One of his latest works, a song cycle of poems by the French poet, Arthur Rimbaud, is a striking work, and makes one hopeful of his future.

Dr. Vaughan Williams may be said to have taken the place of the

46

late Sir Edward Elgar as the head of his profession in England. He is remarkably versatile, having composed operas, symphonies, chamber music, church music and many songs. Of all living English composers he is most deeply imbued with English folk song and the traditional English church music. His *pastoral symphony*, his choral setting of Whitman's verses, a Sea symphony, and many of his songs have given him an assured place in the history of British music.

William Walton has composed chiefly orchestral music. His concerto for viola and orchestra is a work of real talent ; both in it and other compositions, Walton has shown a certain affinity with the contemporary German composer, Paul Hindemith. His choral work, " Belshazzar's Feast," has been one of the most successful of modern English works ; he has also written a symphony and his music to the ballet " Façade," which is one of the most successful in the repertory of Sadler's Wells theatre, is a lively and witty work wholly contemporary in feeling and expression. Peter Warlock, whose real name was Philip Heseltine, was perhaps, next to Vaughan Williams, the composer most influenced by the English tradition. He had a real gift for song and in his short life composed a great number, many of which must be considered among the finest composed in this century.

Dr. Ethel Smyth is the foremost woman composer now living. She studied in Leipzig and was one of Brahms's circle. Her opera, *The Wreckers*, has been often performed in this country and abroad. She has written operas and many instrumental and vocal works.

The annual opera festival at Glyndebourne, Sussex, was started in 1933 and soon rivalled that of the Salzburg festival in Austria. The Glyndebourne opera house was built by Mr. John Christie as an extension to his private house. It holds about 400 people, and is exceptionally well-equipped behind the stage with the most up-to-date machinery and electric stage lighting. Mr. Christie was fortunate in securing the services of Mr. Fritz Busch, who had been the chief conductor at the Dresden Opera House. As producer, he engaged Mr. Carl Ebert. With their co-operation he began with the production of some of Mozart's operas in their original form, with the aid of specially selected casts of singers of all nationalities including English, Welsh and Australian. Special care was taken to rehearse the operas thoroughly and the quality of the productions was far above anything else in the country.

Unfortunately, as this was private enterprise, the prices of seats were extremely high and prohibitive to the majority of people, but it showed what could be done by the right leadership and a rigid adherence to the principle of giving nothing but the best, both with regard to works performed and the performers, and sparing no effort to get as near to perfection as possible in every detail. It is not too much to say that these performances were a revelation to the majority of music lovers who heard them. One might also add that it is impossible for the amateur of music to form any conception of the genius of an operatic composer until his works are performed on the stage with proper understanding and passion. It is likely that the day of the private patron in music is over, but if this is so, it is certain that public enterprise, either municipal or state, will have to take its place, otherwise there will be little hope of the art of music developing, and every chance of its decaying.

The only subsidised opera house in existence in Great Britain and indeed in the British Dominions is that of Sadler's Wells in London. It specialises in performances of both opera and ballet. The British contribution to opera has so far not been great, for reasons which have already been explained, but a very vigorous school of English ballet dancing has been developed in the last twenty-five years, and some celebrated dancers associated with the famous Russian Ballet, conducted by Serge Diaghilev, have affirmed that the English have a natural genius for dancing. Certainly some of the performances of ballet at Sadler's Wells are of a standard not to be surpassed anywhere else in the world at the present time. The ballet is now under the directorship of Ninette de Valois and Frederick Ashton as ballet masters, and a talented English composer, Constant Lambert, is conductor. Sadler's Wells has been privately endowed to some extent by individual benefactors, and it has received this measure of Government support in that it is released from paying the entertainment tax on the grounds of its being an educational institution. This is a step in the right direction. Sadler's Wells now has an extensive repertory and constantly draws large and enthusiastic audiences, but it requires more state assistance in order to improve the standard of its operatic performances. There should be one such subsidised opera house in every city of more than 100,000 inhabitants. The future of English music now depends on the social conditions existing after the present war. The same is certainly true of music in other European countries. In fact, in the present writer's opinion, the chief hope of music lies in a renewal of the general unity in civilization which once prevailed throughout the western world.